Balancing

Risk

Practical strategies to reduce the uncertainty in attaining your business objectives and decrease the frictional cost of managing the four categories of risk faced by all organizations today.

By

Ed Kempkey

Balancing Risk

ISBN-13: 978-1461077244

ISBN-10: 1461077249

Manufactured in the United States of America

First Edition published 2011.

Table of Contents

1. Introduction

"Insanity: doing the same thing over and over again and expecting different results"

Albert Einstein

It happened again. A claim is being reported to the insurance company, and it is going to be an expensive one for the customer. Sure, there is coverage under their policy, but I know from experience it will not pay for everything. On top of that, the loss could easily have been prevented, so this will be a needless waste of money. To make matters worse, I consider this customer to be a good friend, and although we had previously discussed a prevention plan, it was never implemented. I want to do more to help others avoid these costly mistakes.

As an insurance broker for over three decades, I have seen the same situation occur time and time again. While I enjoy a successful practice designing insurance programs and placing coverage, there was a growing sense of dissatisfaction with the impact I was having on my customers' bottom line performance. Any premium savings derived from "shopping" the insurance market for best terms and conditions paled in comparison to the financial leakage resulting from the frictional cost of managing their business risks.

As opposed to the story above, I have now helped many companies avoid these mistakes by going beyond insurance and becoming a student of risk management. By applying some basic techniques, I began to see results that had a measurable impact on reducing my customers' cost of risk. Further research revealed there was an evolution taking place, like the new risk management standard, ISO: 31000, from the International Organization on Standardization (ISO). These innovative concepts and tools are providing new opportunities for the business community to leverage modern best practices and the advantages they offer.

Risk management is a continuous process that needs to begin with identifying the various risks an organization faces. By doing so, it provides a coordinated approach to assessing and responding to all risks that affect the achievement of an organization's strategic and financial objectives.

A successful risk management program is about balance. To be effective, there must be at least one risk control technique and one risk financing technique (typically insurance) for each exposure identified. At the same time, most risk management decisions are financial decisions in that they weigh the benefits of a project with the cost, and should only be undertaken if the benefits outweigh the costs.

If potential risks are not identified, or if one technique is applied without the other, the program is out of balance. If the financial impact is not understood, poor decisions will be made about the proper risk treatments to apply. It is this out of balance condition that prevents the organization from operating at optimum performance. If allowed to continue in this state, the resulting financial loss renders the entity uncompetitive, ultimately losing value.

This book is for mid-size firms which do not have the luxury of employing a full-time risk manager. My purpose is to introduce you to the methodology and latest concepts that can be used to implement an effective program for your firm. You will learn how to develop a written plan using simple tools that will not only guide you through the process, but will allow you to successfully administer the program going forward. You will soon recognize the benefits these best practices have to offer.

Who is This Book For?

This book is for executives at mid-size companies who do not have a full-time risk manager on staff. Experience has shown these are typically organizations with less than 1,000 employees. While everyone should take responsibility for supporting achievement of the organizations objectives, some critical positions could particularly benefit from this book, such as:

- The CEO, who must align the company, internally and externally, with its strategic vision;

- The CFO, who typically has the responsibility for protecting the company against adverse financial results from catastrophic losses;

- Board Members, who are ultimately responsible for oversight of company activities, including risk management;

- Human Resource Professionals, who are charged with overall responsibility for implementing strategies and policies relating to the management of individuals;

- The Safety Officer, who is responsible for monitoring and assessing hazardous and unsafe situations and developing measures to assure personnel safety; and

- Department Managers, who are responsible for reporting all changes in exposure or operations, as well as all losses.

Not only can these individuals benefit from this book, they are the very same people who should take an active role in the implementation process. Modern risk management, as opposed to the traditional approach, is a team effort and has evolved significantly over the past four decades. Historically, an organization's risk management program was transactional in nature. It could be described as being in defensive mode, typically limited to the purchase of insurance in order to transfer risk whenever possible. The individual(s) responsible operated in a silo, with a limited amount of information being shared with other managers, departments, et cetera.

Today, risk management is about identifying threats and opportunities while allowing the organization to optimize performance. Those old silos should be broken down, with the various areas of the organization freely collaborating in their efforts, and generously sharing information.

How Will You Benefit?

As an individual, you will benefit from this book in a number of ways. You will learn the concepts necessary to create a risk management plan, as well as a step by step procedure for implementing the program. This information will also save you time in getting your program up and running.

You may want to share this book with other members of your executive team to encourage communication on the subject in support of your efforts.

And, if you are currently the sole person in your organization tasked with responsibility for risk management, this book should be used to support a case of sharing that responsibility with other members of your management team.

Your organization will benefit as well. According to ISO, when a plan is implemented and maintained, the management of risk enables an organization to, for example:

- increase the likelihood of achieving objectives;
- encourage proactive management;
- be aware of the need to identify and treat risk management throughout the organization;
- improve identification of opportunities and threats;
- comply with relevant legal and regulatory requirements and international norms;
- improve mandatory and voluntary reporting;
- improve governance;
- improve stakeholder confidence and trust;
- establish a reliable basis for decision making and planning;
- improve controls;
- effectively allocate and use resources for risk treatment;
- improve operational effectiveness and efficiency;
- enhance health and safety performance, as well as environmental protection;
- improve loss prevention and incident management;
- minimize losses;

- improve organizational learning; and

- improve organizational resilience.

Whether your organization is non-profit, private, or publicly held company, the material in this book will help you get started on the road to enjoying these and many more benefits.

2. The Need for Risk Management

"There are risks and costs to a program of action. But they are far less than the long-range risks and costs of comfortable inaction."

John F. Kennedy

Some of the driving factors demanding the attention of risk managers today include tort liability costs, regulatory requirements, and emerging risks, all of which generate previously unforeseen costs for business.

Tort Liability Costs

In much of the common law world, the most prominent tort liability is negligence. If the injured party can prove the person believed to have caused the injury acted negligently – that is, without taking reasonable care to avoid injuring others – tort law will allow compensation.

According to the Small Business Administration (SBA), small businesses[1] are significant in number; they employ just over half of all private sector employees, and pay 44 percent of the total U.S. private payroll. A recent U.S. Chamber report[2] found these small businesses bear an extraordinary tort liability cost burden. Their findings are as follows:

- The tort liability price tag for small business in America in 2008 was $105.4 billion.

---

[1] The SBA defines small businesses as having fewer than 500 employees.
[2] U.S. Chamber Institute for Legal Reform, July 2010, *Tort Liability Costs for Small Business.*

- Small businesses bore 81% of business tort liability costs but took in only 22% of revenue.

- Small businesses paid $35.6 billion of their tort costs out of pocket, as opposed to through insurance.

It is interesting to note that more than a third of those surveyed had been sued, and 73% of those sued said the business suffered because the litigation was expensive and very time consuming.

In its most recent report[3], Tillinghast/Towers forecasts future tort costs will reach $183.1 billion in 2011 for all businesses, of which NERA Economic Consulting estimates $152 billion will impact small businesses.

Regulatory Requirements

The flow of federal and state legislation placing regulatory burdens on businesses never seems to end. Examples at the federal level include environmental regulatory requirements covering every aspect of environment protection like air, water, noise, forest conservation, wildlife protection, et cetera. Also, a separate set of laws and rules for emission of hazardous waste have been enacted.

There are many federal laws affecting employment, such as the Family and Medical Leave Act (FMLA), Americans with Disabilities Act (ADA), and OSHA Safety and Health laws, just to name a few. For public companies the Securities and Exchange Commission recently approved rules requiring disclosure about board leadership structure and the board's role in risk oversight.

A recent example at the state level is California Assembly Bill 2774, which became effective January 1, 2011. AB2774 increased the ability of the California Division of Occupational Safety and Health

---

[3] Tillinghast/Towers Perrin, 2009 Update on U.S. Tort Cost Trends.

("Cal/OSHA") to issue citations to employers for "serious violations" of occupational safety and health standards. Some of the key implications for employers include:

- An increase in the number of citations for serious violations issued by Cal/OSHA, along with the attendant penalties.

- A decrease in the success rate of employers appealing citations for serious violations.

- Claims made by injured employees for "serious and willful" injuries, and corresponding increases in workers' compensation benefits, are likely to rise, along with the number of citations for serious violations.

It should be noted that the penalty for "serious and willful" liability is fixed by statute, is an "all or nothing" proposition, and is uninsurable. Other examples of uninsurable claims in many states include punitive damages, wrongful termination stemming from a workers' compensation claim, intentional acts, contract disputes, and damages arising from wage and hour lawsuits.

Emerging Risks

Risks are inherent in every forward-looking business decision, requiring treatments to mitigate their potential future adverse impact to the organization. As the world changes, new risks emerge and must be identified and treated accordingly.

Emerging risks are:

- New exposures to loss for which a risk treatment has not been implemented.

- Existing exposures to loss that are evolving, difficult to quantify, and may have a major financial impact on the organization.

There is a good chance one or more emerging risks are already present within an organization. Common traits include:

- High uncertainty – absence of reliable information; frequency or severity of exposure difficult to predict.

- Difficult to quantify – severity is difficult to forecast; risk transfer techniques may not be suitable for exposure.

- Difficult to communicate – danger of turning areas of concern into "phantom risks" that may not materialize.

- Regulatory involvement – absence of industry response often leads to regulatory involvement.

- No industry position – no one wants to make the first move; adopting a "follower" strategy.

A 2010 survey[4] of 650 executives revealed the top five global emerging risks as follows:

1. Global Recession

2. Regulation Policy Risk

3. Liquidity/Credit Crunch

4. Financial Market Volatility

5. Commodity Price Volatility

Other examples may include dependence on technology, rising medical costs and obesity.

---

[4] Oliver Wyman's "Global Emerging Risk Survey"

3. Risk Management Myths

"A smart man learns from his own mistakes and a wise man from the mistakes of others, but a fool never learns."

Chinese Philosopher

If risk management is such a good business practice, why aren't more organizations taking advantage of it? When asked, managers will give answers that reveal some of the myths about risk management. Some common misconceptions I have heard include:

Five Common Misconceptions

Risk management is only for large companies. While large companies have the advantage of appointing full-time risk management professionals, the risks are the same for small businesses, only on a slightly different scale. Losses do not discriminate based upon the size of a business.

75% of business risks are not covered by insurance.

We have lots of insurance. Insurance is often confused with risk management. Insurance simply transfers the risk to another entity, i.e. the insurance company, and does not cover all the costs associated with a claim. As we will learn in the next chapter, 75% of business risks are not covered by insurance.

We already have a safety program. While safety is an important aspect of risk management, it is just one of many tools available in the process. Most safety programs are built around injury and illness prevention, and fall short on addressing other aspects of the organization's risks, such as disaster planning, supply chain issues, and brand and reputation.

We haven't had any problems so far. This viewpoint from a company assumes that whatever they have done, even if they have done nothing to manage risk, is working well. In other words, if it isn't broken, why fix it? A program based upon luck is truly risky, yet the longer time passes without a problem, the more complacent the organization can become.

It's too expensive to implement a program. Modern techniques and inexpensive tools, such as those presented in this book, make it easy to establish a risk management program. And once implemented, your program's ongoing maintenance requires much less time and money than responding to problems after they occur.

Unrealistic Optimism

The foundation of these misconceptions is revealed in studies that show people tend to think they are invulnerable. Neil Weinstein published his research in this area in an article[5] titled "Unrealistic Optimism About Future Life Events." One of the principal goals of this research was to test the hypothesis that people believe negative events are less likely to happen to them than to others.

In the past, unrealistic optimism about the future was regarded as a defensive phenomenon, a distortion of reality motivated to reduce anxiety. Weinstein's research demonstrated the existence of an optimistic bias concerning future life events as people tend to believe they are more likely than their peers to experience positive events and less likely to experience negative events.

---

[5] N.D. Weinstein, "Unrealistic Optimism About Future Life Events." Journal of Personality and Social Psychology 39, 1980, 806-820

The article goes on to state, "People who believe, falsely, that their personal attributes exempt them from risk or that their present actions reduce their risks below those of other people may be inclined to engage in risky behaviors and to ignore precautions."

Alternatives

Of course, there is a final alternative, and that is to avoid risk altogether. This would involve selling or closing the business. Assuming this is not one of your options, it may be worthwhile to explore risk management and learn about some techniques to increase your risk intelligence.

As a Certified Risk Manager (CRM), I am able to stay up to date on risk management issues through Certified Risk Managers International in association with The National Alliance, and the ongoing educational programs they provide. Much of the information in this book is based upon training I have received from these organizations.

I am also a student of ISO: 31000, referenced by CMA Management as the new gold standard in managing risk. This straightforward global standard, developed by the International Organization for Standardization (named "ISO" which is derived from the Greek isos, meaning "equal"), provides an easy way to get started on implementing a formal risk management plan.

The Short Flight

By the mid-1970's I was selling aircraft insurance in addition to other lines of coverage. This seemed natural since I was a pilot who enjoyed being around airplanes and others who loved flying.

Upon being referred to an aircraft owner in a neighboring city, I agreed to meet at his local airport to discuss his insurance needs. It was a beautiful day, and as I walked across the ramp towards his airplane, I noticed he was preparing to go flying.

It quickly became apparent during our conversation that he did not like insurance and only wanted the minimum that was required. Any effort on my part to explain other options was met by his insistence that in all the years he had been flying, there was never a problem and he was experienced enough to know how to stay out of trouble.

At the time, I was in my mid-twenties and he appeared to be in his late-forties, so out of respect for his "experience" and perceived ideas about insurance, I suggested that he stay with his current insurance provider. It was a short meeting, and after shaking his hand and walking away toward the terminal, I could hear the sound of his engine starting.

I read about the accident the next day in the local newspaper. Shortly after takeoff, the aircraft stalled and crashed into a school yard, destroying the airplane and killing the owner. Fortunately, no one on the ground was injured, and there was no damage to the property of others.

It was an eerie feeling to think that no more than fifteen minutes after I'd shaken hands with this fellow, he was dead. I only hoped that if he had a family, he did not feel the same about life insurance as he did about insuring his airplane.

4. Business Risks

"The only alternative to risk management is crisis management – and crisis management is much more expensive, time consuming, and embarrassing."

James Lam

As mentioned in the introduction, the scope of risk management has expanded considerably in recent years. Once reserved only for hazard risks, it has now expanded to include the full spectrum of risk faced by a business. Modern risk management is more strategic, with an emphasis on optimizing risk by supporting the organization's objectives. It is looked upon as essential in improving earnings and cash flow, managing growth, and capturing opportunities.

Four Categories of Risk

Today, risk management takes a holistic approach and considers risks in four major categories: hazard risks, financial risks, operational risks and strategic risks. It is helpful to review these as we will be referring to them when we learn about risk identification and assessment steps in the risk management process.

The Four Categories of Business Risk

Hazard Risks

Hazard risks include those covered by insurance including natural hazards, physical damage to tangible assets, injury to students, employees and visitors, and environmental impairment. These are commonly referred to as traditional risks.

Financial Risks

Financial risks are related to an organization's financial status, and can include foreign exchange and interest rate, commodity costs, customer default, and equity. Their greatest impact is on the firm's profitability. Following are examples of financial risks:

Credit Risk

Credit risk is associated with a borrower going into default by not making payments as promised. For example, when a customer defaults on a trade invoice, losses include lost principal and interest, decreased cash flow, and increased collections costs. Some companies run a credit check before extending credit. They may use in-house programs or third-party intelligence from companies like Standard & Poor's, Moody's, and Dun and Bradstreet.

Market Risk

Market risk is exposure to the uncertain market value of a portfolio. The four standard market risk factors are stock prices, interest rate, foreign exchange rates and commodity prices.

Equity Risk

Equity risk is the risk that stock prices and/or the implied volatility will change.

Interest Rate Risk

Interest rate risk is the risk that an investment's value will change due to a change in the absolute level of interest rates, in the spread between two rates, in the shape of the yield curve or in any other interest rate relationship.

Currency Risk

Currency risk arises from the change in price of one currency against another. While primarily thought of when companies have assets or business operations across national borders, currency risk exists regardless of whether an organization is investing domestically or abroad. If your investment is in your home country, and your home currency devalues, you have lost money.

Commodity Risk

Commodity risk is the exposure to absolute price changes of commodities (e.g. corn, copper, crude oil) that must be purchased or sold.

Liquidity Risk

Liquidity risk is the risk that arises from the difficulty of selling an asset, typically stemming from the lack of marketability of an investment that cannot be bought or sold quickly enough to prevent or minimize loss.

Operational Risks

Operational risks are those related to processes and management, examples of which include information technology (IT), supply chain issues, brand and reputation, and business interruption. Their greatest impact is on productivity. Following are examples of operational risks.

Information Technology

Most business functions rely on computers and the internet in some capacity. The convenience of using computers is accompanied by many risks, including delays and unexpected costs in development projects, temporary or extended loss of service, data loss or theft, and a myriad of other ills. Also known as IT risks, they increasingly involve public disclosure resulting in reputation damage and regulatory scrutiny. The principal goal of an organization's risk management process should be to protect the organization and its ability to perform its mission, not just to protect IT assets themselves.

Supply Chain

Globalization has led to continuous downward cost pressures and higher customer demands in quality, speed of delivery and overall performance. Companies have embraced just-in-time inventory and other lean manufacturing techniques that emphasize speed and reduced cost. In addition, outsourcing to foreign countries introduces political and currency risks which, combined with cyber attacks and failed communication with suppliers, presents additional challenges. All the while, companies still face traditional property-related risks to their supply chains, such as fire, natural disasters, and equipment breakdowns. All of these risks must be managed in order to prevent supply chain disruptions to continued manufacturing.

Reputation

While reputation is an important corporate asset and can be seen as a major source of competitive advantage, it can also be one of the most difficult assets to protect. A change in the perception of a corporation by the public, suppliers, customers or employees as a result of a business practice, a behavioral incident, or a characteristic of the products sold can have serious financial consequences. One of the biggest threats to reputation is seen to be a failure to comply with regulatory or legal obligations.[6]

"If you lose money for the firm by a bad decision, I will be understanding. If you lose reputation for the firm, I will be ruthless."

Warren Buffet

Business Interruption

Disasters cause enormous damages, yet more than half of all business interruptions are caused by relatively normal events such as power outages, system failures and human error. Some sobering statistics include:

- An estimated 25 percent of businesses do not reopen following a major disaster[7]

- 75% of companies without business continuity plans fail within three years of a disaster[8]

- Of those businesses that experience a disaster and have no emergency plan, 43 percent never reopen; of those

---

[6] Reputation; Risk of Risks, Economist Intelligence Unit, December 2005.
[7] "Open for Business" a publication of The Institute for Business & Home Safety
[8] Bruce Blythe, CEO, Crisis Management International in "Blindsided: A Manager's Guide to Catastrophic Incidents in the Workplace"

that do reopen, only 29 percent are still operating two years later.[9]

Having a disaster recovery plan can be the difference between staying in, or going out of, business. There are many resources available to help a small or growing business make the proper preparations. Disasters are going to happen. The best way to survive is through preparation, and the best way to prepare is to understand this can happen to anyone, including you.

Strategic Risks

Strategic risks will prevent an organization from fulfilling its mission, or cause it to miss opportunities. These include customers, products, channels, competitors, and regulatory issues. The greatest impact is on sales.

According to Adrian Slywotzky, author of The Upside[10], there are seven major kinds of risk for which your business can prepare. They are:

1. Your big initiative fails. What is the true success rate of your company's projects, and how can those odds be changed?

2. Your customers leave you. Has your business ever been surprised by sudden, unforeseen shifts in customer preferences, priorities, and tastes? Have you learned to get inside the minds of your customers, anticipating surprises before they happen?

3. Your industry reaches a fork in the road. When technology or business design shifts transform an industry, as many as 80 percent of incumbent firms fail to survive the transition.

---

[9] The Hartford's Guide to Emergency Preparedness Planning
[10] Adrian J. Slywotzky, *The Upside – The 7 Strategies for Turning Big Threats into Growth Breakthroughs*, Crown Publishing, 2007

4. A seemingly unbeatable competitor arrives. While your business may have yet to encounter a unique competitor, when it does, is it possible to survive and thrive while other companies are being decimated?

5. Your brand loses power. A great brand is supposed to be a fortress of value, yet 40 percent of leading brands experienced significant value erosion in the past five years.

6. Your industry becomes a no-profit zone. Many industries have found themselves suffering from increasing competition, growing customer power, and margin compression until profits are driven practically to zero.

7. Your company stops growing. How can you invent new forms of customer demand that can trigger new waves of growth, even in a seemingly mature industry?

At the end of his book, Slywotzky even provides an outline for a half-day workshop that any management team can use to develop its own strategic risk and upside profile.

Why Businesses Lose Value

While significant, hazard risks only represent 25% of the business risks faced by an organization. Further, surveys show that these types of risks are the least likely to have a negative impact on an organization's value.

It is interesting to note three independent surveys conducted on the reasons for business failures and declining stock prices all reached the same conclusion. Figure 3 displays the results of one of the surveys conducted by Mercer MMC. The leading cause was strategic risk, followed by operational and financial risks. Hazard risk, which attracts all of the attention of risk managers and insurance professionals, was never cited, even though it was one of the survey choices.

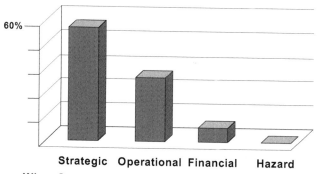

Strategic Operational Financial   Hazard
When Companies Lose Value – Which Risk is Greatest?

Strategic, operational and financial risks have a greater potential to adversely impact an organization's bottom line, and they are not insurable. Their impact shows up in sales, productivity, and financial results. So, if we just focus on the insurance cost of the hazard risks, we may be chasing the wrong rabbit.

"Unmanaged risk is the greatest source of waste in your business and our economy as a whole. Major projects fail; customer shifts make our offers irrelevant; billion-dollar brands erode, then collapse; entire industries stop making money; technology shifts or unique competitors kill dozens of companies in one stroke; companies stagnate needlessly. When these risk events happen, thousands of jobs get lost, brilliant organizations are disassembled, expertise gets lost, and assets are destroyed. Yet all of these risks can be understood, identified, anticipated, mitigated, or reversed, thereby averting hundreds of billions of dollars in unnecessary losses."

Adrian J. Slywotzky
Author "The Upside"

5. The Cost of Risk

"What gets measured gets managed"

Peter Drucker

Ask management about their cost of risk and they will point to the premiums they pay for insurance. This misconception is in part to blame on the insurance industry, for promoting the idea that insurance is risk management. As pointed out earlier in this book, insurance is a form of risk financing, and does nothing to control risk.

Measuring your cost by the amount of premiums paid subjects you to the ups and downs of the insurance industry pricing cycles that alternate between periods of soft and hard conditions. In a hard market, coverage is harder to place and premiums grow. A soft market indicates premiums are stable or falling and coverage may be more readily available. On their own, insurance premiums do not represent a good measure of performance.

In fact, insurance premiums are just one component of the cost of risk, and quite often the smallest part of the company's cost. The Total Cost of Risk (TCOR) concept was first developed over 40 years ago as a yardstick by which to measure the effectiveness of an organization's risk management program. Recognizing all the costs and expenses associated with the risk management function of an organization allows you to do so with credibility.

Components of the Cost of Risk

The four components of TCOR include Insurance Premiums, Taxes & Fees, Administrative Costs, and Loss Costs, both direct and indirect. The sum of these costs represents an organization's TCOR. The next couple of pages will review each of these components and discuss why it is important to know your organization's TCOR. A case study will also be presented to demonstrate its use.

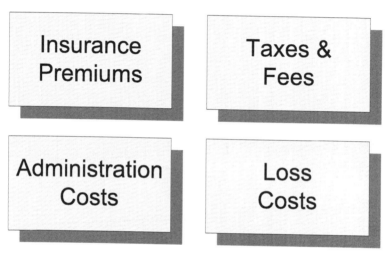

Components of the cost of Risk

Insurance Premiums

For most mid-sized businesses, insurance is the primary form of risk financing. This includes all property, workers' compensation, and liability premiums paid to commercial insurance companies. Any retained losses or high deductible costs must be accounted for in the loss cost component. This aspect of your total cost of risk is readily understandable and easy to compute.

Taxes and Fees

Taxes and fees are simply a function of insurance premiums. An insurance premium tax is a tax upon insurers, both domestic and foreign, for the privilege of engaging in the business of providing insurance. The insurance premium tax doesn't really affect the individual policy holder in a drastic way. Most of the time taxes and fees are invisible unless you are in a self-insured or non-admitted program. Therefore, this second component of TCOR is also very straightforward.

Administrative Expenses

This is the internal administrative cost related to the risk management and insurance department. It includes salaries, training and travel expenses, employee benefits, and other departmental costs. Since most mid-size companies do not have dedicated risk management and insurance departments, these costs may be hard to track and therefore not practical for our purposes.

Loss Costs

This is where the rubber meets the road. Loss costs are the component that truly drives an organization's TCOR, and provide the best source to measure performance. There are two types of loss costs: direct loss costs and indirect loss costs.

Direct Loss Costs

Damage to property, medical and indemnity expenses for an injured employee, and defense costs for a lawsuit are all examples of direct loss costs, and are typically paid by the insurance company. Because we pay a premium (already discussed above and included in our calculation) to transfer these costs to an insurance company, they are not counted in our TCOR. However, another example of direct loss cost is uninsured losses or where a deductible is involved. These are referred to as retained losses, and to the extent feasible should be included in your TCOR calculations.

Indirect Loss Costs

As we will see in a moment, these are the numbers that really drive our TCOR. They are the costs that are not covered by insurance, and contribute heavily to the financial leakage stemming from the various business risks that we discussed in Chapter 4. Several examples include: disruption in production/sales, management time spent on loss-related activities, overtime costs, hiring and training replacement costs, opportunity costs, loss of goodwill and social costs (public image, reputation, etc.).

These productivity robbers have been estimated to be as much as 20 times the direct costs. While these expenses may not be precisely measured, they are real and must be considered in the TCOR calculations in order to measure performance. So how do we recognize them? Read on and I will show you an easy way to do this.

A number of studies have been conducted on the indirect cost of losses. I have included some links to these in the Resource section at the end of this book. The two sources I use when helping clients determine their costs are the Wausau Multiline Productivity Poll, and data from the National Council on Compensation Insurance, Inc.

Wausau's 4th annual Productivity Poll was conducted by Guideline, a national research firm. The 2008 independent survey of 255 financial executives revealed for the first time in four years, more than half of respondents estimate the indirect loss cost to be more than $2 for every $1 of direct loss paid by insurance for general liability, commercial auto, and property claims. Based upon these results, the average for each claim type is displayed in the following chart.

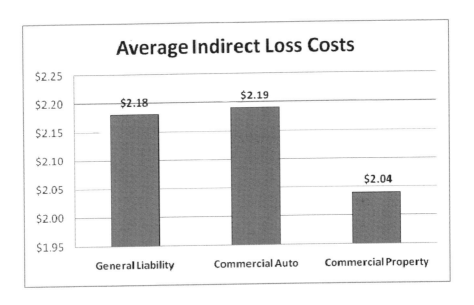

Put another way, these uninsured, indirect loss costs are over and above the direct loss cost paid by insurance. Applying these factors to the amount paid by the insurance company will provide indirect loss costs. A $50,000 general liability claims settlement results in $109,000 in indirect costs ($50,000 x 2.18); while a $10,000 property loss paid by the insurance company results in $20,400 in indirect costs ($10,000 x 2.04). Of course, any deductibles incurred would be over and above these amounts as they would be considered a direct loss cost to the insured.

The National Council on Compensation Insurance, Inc. (NCCI) is the largest provider of workers' compensation insurance and employee injury data and statistics in the United States. The NCCI studies workplace injuries and other national and state factors impacting workers compensation.

The indirect cost estimates provided in this program are based on a study conducted by the Stanford University Department of Civil Engineering. The magnitude of indirect cost is inversely related to the seriousness of the injury. The less serious the injury, the higher the ratio of indirect costs to direct costs (four or five times higher). For more serious injuries, indirect costs will average one or two times the direct costs of the injury. While they account for the majority of the true costs of an accident, indirect costs are usually uninsured and therefore, unrecoverable. An abbreviated listing of INDIRECT COST drivers includes:

- Any wages paid to injured workers for absences not covered by workers' compensation;

- Wage costs related to time lost though work stoppage;

- Administrative time spent by supervisors following accidents;

- Employee training and replacement costs;

- Lost productivity related to new employee learning curves and accommodation of injured employees; and

- Replacement costs of damaged material, machinery and property.

The ratio of indirect to direct costs is displayed in the following graph.

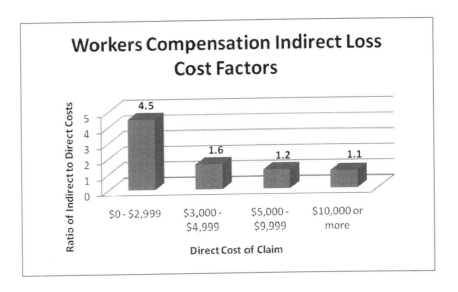

Using these factors, a $2,000 claim paid by the insurance company results in $9,000 in indirect costs borne by the employer, while a $20,000 claim results in $22,000 in indirect loss costs.

Computing Your Real Cost of Risk

Using the indirect loss cost factors from these studies provides a basis upon which you can determine your own organization's factors. Generally speaking, the range for most indirect loss cost factors are somewhere between 2 and 5 times the amount of direct loss costs. While you may adjust the factors up or down based upon your business model, just be sure to be consistent in their application going forward for comparing one period of time to another.

Now, referencing your claims history, use your factors to compute the indirect loss costs, and then enter the amounts for each type of loss on the worksheet in Appendix B. Then enter the cost of deductibles and/or any direct, but uncovered, cost of your claims. Finally, enter the premiums paid for each line of coverage, sum the columns, and total the sums to compute your Total Cost of Risk.

Why it is Important to Know Your Cost of Risk

We measure all aspects of our business in order to make the adjustments necessary to optimize performance. The same holds true for our risk management program. Understanding your cost of risk is critical for making effective risk management decisions, establishing and measuring progress toward risk management objectives, and providing incentives to support the effort. By communicating the financial impact of a loss on the cost of risk and sales revenue, we can better focus members of our team on promoting safety and loss control.

Making Effective Risk Management Decisions

Most risk management decisions are financial decisions, in that they weigh the benefits of a project with the cost, and should only be undertaken if the benefits outweigh the costs. Whether in purchasing a security system, creating standards, policies and administrative controls, or implementing a training program, knowing the costs can help us make the best decision.

For example, if we are incurring workplace injuries as a result of lifting, and we know what these types of injuries are costing our company in both direct and indirect loss costs, then it is easy to decide on investing in lifting devices and/or ergonomic programs in order to reduce or eliminate these costs.

Measuring Progress Toward Risk Management Objectives

Benchmarking is commonly thought of as the process of comparing one's business performance metrics to industry bests and/or best practices from other industries. However, it can also be used to compare different periods of time in order to track trends within the same company. By recognizing all of the costs, then using a common denominator like revenue, a common unit of measurement allows one to determine a rate per thousand dollars of sales. While costs and revenues fluctuate from year to year, the rate puts it all into proper perspective.

Once a benchmark period is established, subsequent comparison periods can be used to track these rates over time to identify trends in the effectiveness of the risk management program.

Providing Management and Employee Incentives

By understanding the total cost of risk, we can establish an allocation system to attribute the costs to various departments, stores, projects or other accounting units. The objectives include creating accountability and enhancing loss control.

Bonuses, salary increases, and performance evaluations tied to the allocation system create employee awareness of the costs associated with losses and exposures, and help identify those locations, managers, employees and environments in need of risk management attention. This approach also motivates personnel to reduce loss frequency and severity, and makes managers accept ownership for losses.

Impact of a Loss on Cost of Risk and Sales/Revenue

Dividing the loss costs by the organization's profit margin, we can determine the sales or revenue required to pay for the losses. The following chart displays the amount of sales/revenue required to pay for various amounts of loss cost.

Loss Cost	Profit Margin				
	1%	2%	3%	4%	5%
$1,000	$100,000	$50,000	$33,333	$25,000	$20,000
$5,000	$500,000	$250,000	$166,666	$125,000	$100,000
$10,000	$1,000,000	$500,000	$333,333	$250,000	$200,000
$25,000	$2,500,000	$1,250,000	$833.333	$625,000	$500,000
$100,000	$10,000,000	$5,000,000	$3,333,333	$2,500,000	$2,000,000

Referencing the above chart, a company with a 5% profit margin that incurs a $10,000 loss will have to make an additional $200,000 in sales to cover the cost. Which is easier for an organization to accomplish: preventing a loss of $10,000, or increasing sales or revenue by $200,000?

TCOR in Action

I completed a risk assessment for a well established beverage manufacturer which resulted in the implementation of an action plan to mitigate the top five risks over a twelve month period. At the same time, the CFO decided to begin tracking their TCOR as part of measuring their progress..

The CFO decided to use loss cost factors based upon the median cost of three years' data from the Wausau Multiline Productivity Poll. Also, since most workers' compensation claims were under $10,000, he decided to apply a single factor to all of the workers' compensation claims. The following quantifiable data and cost multipliers were established:

Coverage:	Indirect Loss Cost Factor*:
Workers' Compensation	1.20
General Liability	1.61
Automobile	1.52
Property	1.56

* *Factor to be multiplied times the direct loss amount paid by the insurance company.*

The first six months of our action plan was devoted to writing the policies, standards, and procedures that would be used to mitigate the risks. During the latter six months we implemented the programs, two of which were for workplace safety and vehicle safety—the areas where they had been experiencing losses.

At the end of the second year, we compared the results of the current year (comparison period, with the risk mitigation techniques in place) with the prior year (benchmark period before we had instituted these risk control measures). Using the agreed indirect loss cost factors gave us the following:

	Benchmark Period	Comparison Period
Total Indirect Loss Cost:	$285,653	$88,936
Sales:	$64,600,000	$60,000,000
Rate Per $1,000 (Sales)	$4.42	$1.48

The indirect loss cost component rate difference was computed by subtracting the comparison period rate from the benchmark period rate. The difference of $2.94 was multiplied by the comparison period sales to determine the savings. This figure was then used against a 6% profit margin to show the impact on sales. Here is the math:

Indirect Loss Cost Savings: $4.42 - $1.48 = $2.94 x $60,000 = $176,400

Impact on Sales: $176,400 ÷ .06 = $2,940,000

In addition to the indirect loss cost, we would add the insurance premiums paid for each period to determine our total cost of risk. If the insurance market prices were rising, the savings on the indirect loss cost component would help by offsetting the premium increase. And if prices were falling, the reduction in loss cost would compound the savings.

In either event, once the proper mitigation techniques are put in place, the organization will enjoy sustainable cost reductions going forward, adding up to even more significant savings over time.

I would like to thank my good friend, Rob Ekern, for the concepts that have been shared in this chapter. His company, C.R. Ekern & Company, is North America's leading consultancy for professionals looking to master the Total Cost of Risk and help their clients manage business risks. I have learned much from his knowledge and experience.

6. The Risk Management Process

"I learned to embrace risk, as long as it was well thought out and, in a worst-case scenario, I'd still land on my feet"

Eli Broad

Wouldn't it be great if there were a process you could follow to manage your organization's risks? Fortunately, there is not only a logical, systematic process, but also a simple method that can be used to document your progress. This chapter will introduce you to both the process and the plan document to help jump-start your program. Before we dive into the details, let's take a moment to define an important term, *risk*, and how it applies to this methodology.

According to Dictionary.com, "risk" is defined as, "An exposure to the chance of injury or loss; a hazard or dangerous chance: *It's not worth the risk.*"

Wikipedia.com defines "risk" as, "The variability in possible outcomes, usually in reference to the possibility of negative results."

Contained within the new international risk standard, ISO:31000 from the International Organization for Standardization (ISO), "risk" is defined as, "Effect of uncertainty on objectives."

Each of these sources includes a common thread of uncertainty or probability. For simplicity's sake, I like the definition put forth by Certified Risk Managers International, which is:

"Uncertainty concerning a loss arising out of a given set of circumstances."

They go further to say the definition of risk management is:

"The process of protecting an organization's assets through exposure identification, exposure analysis, controlling exposures, financing losses with external and internal funds, and the implementation and monitoring of the risk management process."

Consider also the fact that there are two types of risk: pure and speculative. Pure risks are those where there is only a chance of loss, while speculative risks have the possibility of loss or gain. The process described below can be used to address pure risks only (traditional risk management) or pure *and* speculative risks (enterprise risk management).

Four Step Process

The risk management process involves four steps: risk identification, risk assessment, implementation of solutions, and monitoring results. The process is continuous, as depicted in the following graphic.

The Risk Management Process

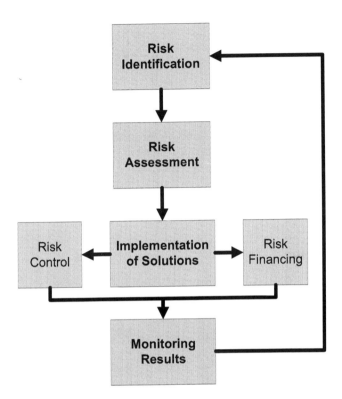

Identify Risks

This is the first and most important step in the process since an unidentified risk cannot be analyzed, controlled, or financed, and leaves the organization exposed to loss. In Chapter 8 we will look at the various methods for identifying risks, as well as how to state each risk so it receives the proper treatment.

Assess Risks

Chapter 9 will take us through the second step in the process, which is prioritizing the identified risks. By ranking the risks and assessing the current controls in place, we are able to make the best informed decisions about which risks we can tolerate and upon which ones we must take action.

Implement Solutions

Once we gain a better understanding of the risks, we can implement appropriate solutions. In Chapter 10 we will learn about the seven root causes within management's control in order to develop strategies to improve safety, reliability, quality, and financial performance.

Monitor Results

In Chapter 11 we will see how to track the status of your risk mitigation efforts, including a system of accountability for implementation. We will also see how we can document our decisions using a risk register to improve governance as well as stakeholder confidence and trust.

The Blame Game

This story is about one of my early attempts at helping a company assess their risks. It involved a manufacturer which was experiencing frequent workplace accidents. The problem was not confined to any one area, as my analysis of their claims history showed that all departments were incurring losses, particularly involving injuries to employees. This was driving up the cost of their workers' compensation insurance. The CEO agreed to hold a meeting with the management team so we could discuss ideas to mitigate the problem.

I came to the meeting prepared with my analysis and suggestions, based upon individual interviews and having reviewed certain safety documents, mostly noting the important documents that did not exist. I was honored that the CEO invited me to sit at the head of the table next to her, and after a very short introduction, she turned the meeting over to me.

As I recall, my presentation lasted less than two minutes, and only introduced the fact that injury claims were at an unacceptable level and occurring in all departments. There were about a dozen department managers in the meeting, and one by one they pointed at one another's departments as being the source of the problem. After a few minutes of this blame game, I thought the CEO would chime in and get the meeting back on course—but that did not happen.

While the brawl was continuing, I closed up my presentation material and waited until it was appropriate to excuse myself. There were no follow up meetings and the losses continued for years to come. I learned then that without leadership from top management, there is little hope for success in developing a risk management program, not to mention just trying to take the first step with a group of adults to intelligently assess their organization's risks.

7. Getting Organized

"The way to get started is to quit talking and begin doing"

Walt Disney

Before launching into the risk management process, we need to take some time to get organized. This chapter will discuss how to establish a risk management committee, and the tools you will need to work through the four-step process.

Risk Management Committee

Recall from Chapter 1 that modern risk management no longer operates in a silo; it is conducted as a team effort that promotes communication and shared responsibility. There are numerous ways to identify and assess risk, such as interviews, questionnaires, checklists and documentation review. While these can be used to supplement the process, the suggested method is to establish a risk management committee. Usually, involving a group of people is best because:

1. It encourages participation and gets more people involved in the process.

2. It increases the amount of time and energy participants are able to give.

3. It enhances the visibility and stature of the process.

4. It provides a broad perspective on the issues.

A risk management committee supports a team effort that taps into the collective wisdom of participants to develop a truly effective plan. To be successful, the committee should have a written charter that includes the following:

- Purpose – why does the committee exist?

- Membership – who will comprise the committee?

- Chairman – who will chair the committee?

- Meetings – when and how often will the committee meet?

- Responsibilities – what functions will be undertaken?

- Authority – what information is accessible and what functions can be delegated?

- Reporting – to whom does the committee report?

A sample risk management committee charter is displayed in Appendix C. The largest workable team usually has a core group of about eight, however four to six is the optimum number. It is best that members of the committee be from the same level of management. If you engage in identifying risks in specialized areas, you can include a subject matter expert on the team.

In addition to the standing risk committee, you can also facilitate an ad hoc committee in a separate session, confined to a different level of management, for purposes of assessing risks in a specific area or department, like production. You may find people closer to the "action" may identify risks of which upper management was previously unaware, and have some good ideas for mitigating those risks. This also supports good communication and teamwork.

Risk Register

The risk register is a management tool used to record identified risks and action plans. We use a spreadsheet divided into three main sections: risk identification, risk assessment, and risk management. An example is displayed in Appendix D, and may be downloaded from www.riskskillscenter.com. The first section, for recording the identified risks, includes two columns: one for the risk category and the other for stating the risk. These will be explained in Chapter 8, Identifying Risks.

The second section, Assessing Risks, has six columns that allow us to rank the importance of each risk, comment on the extent of current controls in place, and make decisions on how we will tolerate the situation. Completing this section will be reviewed in Chapter 9, Assessing Risk.

The third section of our risk register is about managing risk, and has one column to record the solutions to be implemented to mitigate the risks; details of this section are covered in Chapter 10, Implementing Solutions. The other three columns in this section are devoted to tracking our progress, including who owns the risk, the current status, and date for completion. These will be covered in Chapter 11, Monitoring Results.

So, as we examine each step in the risk management process over the next four chapters, we will also be referring to the risk register and how to complete each of these sections while developing your plan. We will be demonstrating the application through examples, but keep in mind that you can define columns in your risk register to suit your particular business needs.

Also, keep in mind that the risk register is a "living document". By that, I mean it will be continually edited and updated over time as your ability to identify new risks expands.

Getting Started

The areas of risk to be covered should be decided by management and made clear to all participants before undertaking the project. You can choose to focus on a single risk category (see Appendix E for examples) or several categories of risk. For example, you can focus on risks that cause injuries to employees, or, if you are a non-profit, the risks associated with resource development. It is recommended that strategic risks should be assessed on their own and not in conjunction with other areas of risk.

Designating a Facilitator

The designated facilitator should keep participants focused on the categories of risk to be considered, and follow the risk register in developing the plan. This individual should be good at asking high-quality questions that elicit input from participants. It is also a good idea to appoint an assistant who can enter information into the risk register.

Once these three pieces are put in place, a short training session should be conducted by the facilitator to include:

- An overview of the process
- Risk categories to be considered
- Instructions on how to state a risk
- The details of the risk prioritization system
- How to describe existing controls

- Proper tolerance and decision taxonomy

These items can be covered by reference to this book and the handouts available for download at www.RiskSkillsCenter.com.

After the briefing, the process can begin with brainstorming. The risk register can be displayed on a computer monitor, with the responses typed in as received from participants. Tips for eliciting input from participants are covered in the following chapters.

8. Identifying Risks

"It's tough to make predictions, especially about the future."

Lawrence Peter ("Yogi") Berra

Imagine an air traffic controller trying to separate airliners departing and arriving at Chicago's O'Hare International airport without being able to see their location on the radar screen. He or she would not know whether to instruct left or right turns, or give climb or descend commands in order to avoid collisions; ultimately, there would be a disaster.

So it is with risks that are unknown to your organization. If not identified, you cannot treat them. Therefore, identifying risks is considered the most important step in the risk management process. The first two columns of our risk register help us get started on the process by categorizing risks and stating them in a consistent manner.

Risk Categories

The purpose of categorizing risks is twofold. First, categorizing risks helps us to think about the types of risks that might be identified. Second, it sets the stage for focusing on the areas of risk that were agreed upon before starting the process. Providing a list of risks by category to each participant at the beginning of the process will prompt discussions that lead to identifying risks whether they are on the list or not.

You can start by using the four categories of business risks that were discussed in Chapter 4, or you can narrow it down to a single category, like operational risks if that is the area you want to emphasize. Another example would be to consider specific subject matter categories that may be appropriate to participants who are experts in their field. Information technology, environmental, and security risks are examples of categories in specialized areas.

The main idea at this point is to generate a comprehensive list of risks that will be assessed as you move through the process. To further stimulate your thinking, several examples of risk categories and the types of risks you may want to consider are presented in Appendix E.

Risk Statements

We now move to the Risk Statement column of the risk register, where we will frame the risk in terms of its root cause and the consequences, thereby setting the stage for further analysis of the risk and development of the appropriate risk control response later in the process.

For example, if we state the risk as "We could experience an earthquake (a natural hazard category risk) at our facility," there is no specific response from a risk control perspective to address it. On the other hand, if the risk were stated as, "Without a business continuity plan, our recovery from an earthquake or other natural disaster could be prolonged to the point of losing market share," now we have something to talk about. The root cause of the prolonged recovery is the fact that we are not prepared with a business continuity plan (also referred to as a disaster plan). The consequences for this are serious, perhaps to the point of being unable to re-enter the market.

But how do we think in "root cause" terms, to properly state our risks? The easiest way I know of is to take a lesson from the world of incident (accidents and near-misses) investigation.

One of the best courses I have found on the subject is "Root Cause Analysis and Incident Investigation" by ABS Consulting[11]. This three day workshop helps attendees initiate a root cause analysis incident investigation and develop appropriate recommendations to avoid future incidents. While the methodology is presented for use on a reactive basis, it can also be applied on a proactive basis to help formulate risk statements and ultimately prevent losses.

The handbook[12] that comes with the course (and can be purchased separately), contains some definitions that are helpful in formulating risk statements. To begin with, root causes are deficiencies of management systems, and must be within the control of management to address. In our earlier example, we cannot control the occurrence of an earthquake at our facility; however, we do have control over utilizing our management system to develop and implement a disaster recovery plan.

Management systems are put in place to encourage desirable behaviors and discourage undesirable behaviors. Examples include policies, procedures, training, communications, protocols, design methods and codes and standards. The handbook goes on to say:

> "Virtually every incident can be prevented by developing and implementing appropriate management systems. Even in instances where individual personnel performance issues e.g, drug abuse, malicious acts, lack

---

[11] www.ABSConsulting.com/TrainingServices
[12] Root Cause Analysis Handbook, ABS Consulting

of attention, reasoning capabilities) are a cause of an incident, the management systems that are used to select, train, and supervise personnel should be reviewed to determine whether improvements are necessary. In many cases, the individual performance is a direct result of the management systems in place. Therefore, the absence, neglect, or deficiencies of management system features are fundamentally the root cause of nearly all incidents."

ABS Consulting traces the root cause of incidents to one of two categories, each of which contains several root causes. They are expressed as follows:

Company Standards, Policies and Administrative Controls (SPAC) Issue.

- No SPAC or issue not addressed in SPAC

- SPAC not strict enough

- SPAC confusing or contradictory

- SPAC incorrect

Company Standards, Policies and Administrative Controls (SPAC) Not Used.

- Unaware of SPAC

- SPAC recently changed

- SPAC enforcement issue

Policies are the most general types of documents and are statements about how different types of activities will be performed. Standards describe the methods used to measure acceptable performance against the policy. Procedures are step by step documents that describe how a task will be accomplished. Finally, records or proof documents provide evidence that the policies and procedures are implemented and standards are being met.

While this is an abbreviated discussion about root causes, you can use these terms as a starting point to develop your risk statements. The trick is to ask why a risk exists until the answer contains both a root cause and the consequences of not addressing that cause. Following are examples of some risk categories and corresponding risk statements I have seen on risk registers:

Risk Category	Risk Statement
Automobile Liability	Driver acceptability standards only address new hires and not existing employees, resulting in a vehicle being driven by an employee with a suspended or revoked drivers license, or otherwise poor record while on business, thereby exposing the company to punitive damages in the event of an accident.
Liability	Failure to secure proof of insurance from subcontractors, vendors, lessees, or suppliers leads to loss for which they are responsible, yet which ends up on our insurance and loss record.
Hazard	Irregular interval of time between flow testing our fire suppression system leads to undetected failure, rendering the sprinkler system useless at the time of need.
Business Interruption	Lack of a business continuity plan could prolong our recovery in the event of fire or other natural disaster, resulting in substantial lost revenue and potential loss of market share.
Claims Management	Inconsistent use of our return to work programs between departments' increases costs associated with workplace injuries.

A final source for generating ideas to create a list of risks would be the form 10-K of other, publicly-traded firms in your industry. In the Form 10-K, or annual financial report, you can refer to Section 9 where they must publicly disclose their identified risks. Some of these are very interesting and may stimulate your thoughts about risks previously not considered.

Now that we have identified our risks, it is time to analyze them in order to establish priorities. The next chapter will lead us through this part of the process and show us how to further document our plan.

Perfect Timing

A manufacturer of high quality products had already identified several risks and was aware of the need to put some controls in place to manage them. One individual was tasked with creating a calendar to establish dates when each of the risk mitigation measures would be completed. She asked what I thought of the way she prioritized the projects.

After commending her and her company for this undertaking, I asked her a few questions. The first question was how they arrived at the list of identified risks, which at that time was only about five in total. She said they had a couple of management meetings where these issues were brought up, and recognized it was time to do something about them. At this point, it was an informal process, but they were committed to moving forward with the project.

My next couple of questions were about how they assessed these risks in order to establish priorities, and what mitigation plans had been contemplated. Since they were still trying to line up the projects using the calendar, and had not yet determined how to treat the risks, I suggested a more formalized approach: using the risk management process and recording it on a risk register.

The timing was perfect, as they were committed and embraced the idea of moving forward with better direction. To make a long story short, we completed the process and established an action plan. Some of the original risks they contemplated ranked as high priority, while others did not even make the top 20. This story goes back several years, and I recently had a meeting with their eight person management team to offer ideas for a risk mitigation that is scheduled to be completed. They are still working the plan by retiring completed risks and adding new ones.

Perhaps the lesson here is the importance of timing, which certainly plays a role in many decisions as to when an organization can undertake certain projects. The importance of managing risk is evident; however it is easy to delay plans to get started. The question is, therefore, when will you commit to a time to get started on managing risk?

9. Assessing Risks

"When everyone feel that risks are at their minimum, over-confidence can take over and elementary precautions start to get watered down"

Ian Macfarlane

At this point in the process you have probably come up with a considerable list of risks. Before you can make informed decisions about how to respond to these risks, you need to prioritize them and identify areas requiring further analysis.

Prioritizing risk is accomplished by considering a combination of the likelihood and consequences of each risk. Risk mapping is a key management tool to prioritize risks as it is easy to understand and facilitates dialogue concerning risk. The following is an example of risk mapping describing the relationship between likelihood and consequences[13].

Scale from Guidelines for Managing Risk in the Western Australian Public Sector

	Consequences				
Likelihood	*Extreme*	*High*	*Medium*	*Low*	*Negligible*
Almost Certain	Severe	Severe	High	Major	Trivial
Likely	Severe	High	Major	Significant	Trivial
Moderate	High	Major	Significant	Moderate	Trivial
Unlikely	Major	Significant	Moderate	Low	Trivial
Rare	Significant	Moderate	Low	Trivial	Trivial

---

[13] Guidelines for Managing Risk in the Western Australian Public Sector, The Government of Western Australia 1999

Likelihood and consequences should be viewed not only within the context of current controls, which may detect or prevent undesirable risks and events, but also in the absence of such controls.

Likelihood

Likelihood is the probability of something happening. For this purpose, it is a way of expressing knowledge or belief that the risk will occur. Expressing likelihood on a numerical scale, with corresponding descriptions of each point on the scale, allows us to assign a score for rating the probability of the risk occurring. The following is an example of a table utilizing the numerical scale and corresponding descriptions for likelihood.

Adapted from Guidelines for Managing Risk in the Western Australian Public Sector

| Likelihood: The probability that the risk event will occur ||
Numerical Scale	Keyword Descriptor
5	Almost certain
4	Likely
3	Moderate
2	Unlikely
1	Rare

Consequences

Consequences are the effect, result, or outcome of something happening earlier. For our purposes, it is a way of signifying the degree of severity of the risk event. Similar to likelihood, we can express consequences on a numerical scale, with corresponding descriptions of each point on the scale, thereby allowing us to assign a score for rating the severity resulting from the risk occurring. The following is an example of a table utilizing the numerical scale and corresponding descriptions for consequences.

Scale from Guidelines for Managing Risk in the Western Australian Public Sector

Consequence: the degree of severity of the risk event	
Numerical Scale	**Keyword Descriptor**
5	Extreme
4	High
3	Medium
2	Low
1	Negligible

We can expand either of these tables if it is helpful to do so. For example, in the likelihood table we can add a column next to the keyword descriptors with a range of percentages for each point on the scale. Or, in the consequence table, we can add a column with a range of dollars that are attached to each point on the scale. The important thing here is to provide appropriate information to assist in your decisions about scoring the risks.

It is also important at this stage to allow each participant to rate the risks without influence from others. This can be accomplished by printing the first four columns of your risk register and distributing them for each person to write in their scores in the appropriate likelihood and consequence columns. These "scorecards" can then be collected and tallied to arrive at an average score that can be entered into your risk register. By completing the two score columns, and using our examples of risk categories and statements from the last chapter, our risk register would now look like the following:

Risk Category	Risk Statement	L	C
Automobile Liability	Consequences for not meeting company driver acceptability standards are not clear, resulting in vehicles being driven by an employee with a suspended or revoked drivers license, or otherwise poor record, while on company business, thereby exposing the company to punitive damages in the event of an accident.	2	5
Liability	Failure to secure proof of insurance from subcontractors, vendors, lessees, or suppliers leads to loss for which they are responsible yet ends up on our insurance and loss record.	3	5
Hazard	Irregular intervals of time between flow testing our fire suppression system leads to undetected failure, rendering the sprinkler system useless at the time of need.	4	5
Business Interruption	Lack of a business continuity plan could prolong our recovery in the event of fire or other natural disasters, resulting in substantial lost revenues and potential loss of market share.	4	5
Claims Management	Inconsistent use of our return to work programs between department's increases costs associated with workplace injuries.	2	4

Risk Ranking

The next column on the risk register is the score, which is simply the number arrived at by multiplying the likelihood numerical value times the consequences numerical value. We can then rank these scores using a description that draws attention to their relative importance. The risk register used in our example contemplates the following four levels of risk for ranking purposes:

Score	Level
20 – 25	Extreme
11– 19	High
6 - 10	Medium
1 - 5	Low

Existing Controls

Controls are often thought of as an element of management accounting. Recall from Chapter 8 that it is company standards, policies and administrative controls that comprise management systems, and it is the absence, neglect, or deficiencies of these management system features that are the root cause of nearly all incidents.

Controls should be characterized by a key word (for example, "non-existent", "insufficient", or "satisfactory") and documented briefly in the risk register. As mentioned earlier, the quality of existing controls should be taken into account when considering likelihood and consequence ratings.

Tolerance-Decision

The course of action in responding to a particular risk can be expressed as a combination of our capacity for enduring the risk, and making a judgment on how to proceed. This is expressed in the tolerance-decision column of the risk register and can be articulated using certain descriptive key words.

Tolerance can be described as low, medium, or high, while decision key words could include monitor, avoid, or treat.

At this point, the risk assessment section of our risk register should look like the following:

L	C	Score	Rank	Controls	Tolerance-Decision
2	5	10	Medium	Weak: Current standard does not address consequences	Low - Treat
3	5	15	High	Non-existent: No procedure in place to manage certificates of insurance.	Medium - Treat
4	5	20	Extreme	Weak: No written procedure or documented tests.	Low - Treat
5	4	20	Extreme	Non-existent: No plan currently in place.	Low - Treat
2	4	8	Medium	Adequate: Plan is in place but needs training	High - Monitor

Now it is time to move on to the risk management section of our risk register and implement the appropriate solutions to risks we have assessed thus far.

10. Implementing Solutions

*"The bitterness of poor quality lasts long
after the sweetness of cheap price"*

Anonymous

Having identified and assessed the risks, we are now ready to decide on the techniques to be used in managing the highest priority items. An effective risk management program uses at least one risk control technique and one risk financing technique (typically insurance) for each identified exposure. When one of these techniques is applied without the other, I refer to the program as being out of balance and exposing the organization to financial loss. The title of this book reflects a balanced, and therefore effective, risk management program. This chapter provides concepts that will assist in deciding on the proper solutions to implement for each of these techniques.

Taking Ownership

Sometimes it is hard to get all members of a management team together at one time. On this particular project, all six of the executives showed up for the first meeting, and each seemed eager to get started. They were all under forty years old, and as it turned out, each held an equal amount of stock in the company.

It generally took half of the first meeting to explain the process and the concepts that would be used. This group grasped the ideas quickly, and before long we were identifying risks. As a facilitator, I generally find I have to coax people into stating risks at this stage, but not with this group. So it went with the rest of the project, and they even came up with a couple of risk categories I had never thought of.

Nothing against older, meaning mature, people (I am one), but this group was fun to work with and continues to innovate. To this day they are still tackling risks and demonstrating leadership in their marketplace.

Risk Financing

Risk financing can be described as structuring the availability of funds, either internally or externally, to cover the financial effect of unexpected losses experienced by the organization. The methods used to accomplish this range from fully self-insured plans, where the entity retains responsibility to bear these costs, to fully-insured plans where the entity transfers the financial responsibility to an insurance company.

Retention, where we are using internal funds to pay losses, may be active or passive. Active retention is planned, and may include such techniques as current expensing, funded reserves, or borrowing. On the other hand, passive retention is unplanned, and may be attributed to a failure to identify exposures or sources of loss, or to act on a known exposure. Consequently, there is no such thing as an uninsured loss. An uninsured loss is retention.

Depending on the severity, passive retention can be devastating, and points again to the importance of using a process to manage risk. As discussed in Chapter 5, the first step of the process, identifying risk, is the most important step in avoiding these unplanned surprises. Our risk register does not have a column for risk financing, as this is typically addressed with an insurance checklist. You can, however, include a column if you want to make a notation about the status of your financing decision.

Very large organizations have the means to retain a large portion of their risks, and can typically afford full-time risk managers to assist in considering alternative risk financing solutions. Most readers of this book are involved in businesses of the size that rely on insurance as their primary risk financing technique. There are plenty of books on the subject of insurance, and a good broker should serve as your primary resource for information on the insurance marketplace, coverage options, etc., so it is not the intent of this book to go into depth on these issues.

However, there is a point I would like to make about choosing an insurance company. I believe the insurance industry, both carriers and brokers, has done a disservice to buyers by focusing so much of their attention on price, when in fact the purchase of insurance involves complex, highly differentiated solution alternatives. Making the decision solely based upon price assumes insurance is a commodity, with no difference between financial strength, stability, coverage, or service. I share the following three short stories to illustrate my point.

Only the Best

In 1978 I was recruited to be the Vice President of Underwriting for a Southern California insurance company that specialized in insuring trucking companies. Up until then, most of my experience was that of an independent broker, spending my time out in the field selling insurance to these truckers. As a result, I was quite familiar with the industry and who were the good and bad players in the transportation world. The difference at that point was that I was a stockholder and officer in the insurance company, and my role was to select and price the insurance for these trucking companies based upon their risk characteristics so we could make a profit.

Taking this responsibility seriously, I reviewed applications for insurance from other brokers who were requesting quotes. Our rate structure was quite competitive based upon meeting certain underwriting guidelines, so we only accepted those risks that operated with the best practices.

Things were going well until the insurance company's growth leveled off in 1980. I was told that to increase market share, we had to either reduce rates or lower our standards for acceptance into the program. Now I am not an actuary, so calculating an adequate rate was beyond me, but I did know the market, and the idea of accepting risks that were below average did not seem appropriate.

To make a long story short, my decision to decline applications for truckers who did not meet our criteria was overridden by management's desire for growth. This ultimately forced me to make a decision about my future with the company (a tough one, especially since I had invested money in it), and I chose to resign in July of 1980.

Within two years the insurance company was declared insolvent. Friends who stayed with the insurance company told me about the day that the department of insurance escorted them out of the building while locksmiths changed the keys. That was the end of what started to be a great concept of insuring the best risks in a certain industry.

Nice Rugs

In 1984 I had an appointment with the marketing department of an insurance company in San Francisco. The reason for the meeting was to talk about representing them as a broker since at the time they were offering extremely competitive rates. Sitting in the fancy waiting room, I could not help but notice what appeared to be expensive rugs everywhere. Soon I was being escorted into one of the conference rooms and sure enough, there were not only more expensive rugs, but also what appeared to be gold plated fixtures on the walls and the ceiling. I remember touching the wall to see if all of the wood was real – it was.

After the meeting I had a strange feeling about this company. How could they offer such low rates and still afford to operate out of such luxurious offices? It just did not make sense, ultimately resulting in my deciding not to represent them. That decision was proven correct when insolvency proceedings began with a court ordered conservation in 1985. There went another one down the drain.

Left on the Dock

I had planned a visit with the claims department of a Northern California workers' compensation insurance company to review some open claims for one of our customers. During the meeting I noticed that there were claim files stacked in the hallways, against walls in cubicles, and everywhere else I looked. I asked the claims examiner what was going on and she said that they had some layoffs and the workload was backed up. This was cause for concern since I had placed most of my customers with this company because of their excellent claims service.

At the same time, I noticed that the underwriting department was offering deals that seemed too good to be true. This resulted in fast growth, as it attracted a lot of new business with low rates, placing even more strain on the claims department. I called the marketing department about my concerns and was transferred over to one of the vice presidents, who suggested we have lunch and discuss the situation. His explanations during our lunch meeting were not satisfying, and detecting this, he made the statement that the ship was leaving the dock, and I was either on it or not. Not liking his tone, or his explanations, I let him know that I was choosing to stay on the dock.

Our lunch ended quickly, but it took another eighteen months for the ship to sink. In the meantime, we moved all our customers out of that company, and I felt fortunate to have dodged yet another bullet.

One of the people I have followed for years is Chris Burand of Burand & Associates, LLC. Chris consults with agents and brokers on a variety of topics, one of which is the importance of carrier stability. In his annual Property and Casualty Insurance Carrier Growth, Market Share & Stability Report, he points out that a carrier's claims paying rating (i.e., A.M. Best ratings) does not necessarily indicate future stability or future problems.

Chris expends considerable effort to analyze insurance carrier growth, which he believes to be the key indicator of company stability. His analyses have shown companies as extremely unstable 6 months to 4 years before any rating company began their claims rating downgrade process. Aside from the obvious problems with negative growth, he points to sudden, fast growth as an indicator of stability issues. This typically happens when a carrier lowers its rate in an effort to gain market share.

These findings are consistent with a recent Impairment Review Special Report from A.M. Best that revealed over 50% of insurer impairments were due to deficient loss reserves, inadequate pricing, and rapid growth.

I am not trying to downplay the idea of getting a good price, but rather to encourage the importance of making an informed decision that provides the best value. Here are some questions you may want to ask when considering a carrier:

Questions	Considerations
How long has the insurance company been in business?	New or recent entrants have no track record by which to judge performance. Also, they may under-price to build market share, leading to stability problems down the road.
How long has the insurance company been doing business in your geographical area?	Carriers have been known to come in and out of states based upon regulatory climate and profitability. Longer term is preferable, as it demonstrates commitment to the area.
How long has the insurance company been doing business with your industry?	Same as above, as it applies to industries. Longer term demonstrates commitment and industry knowledge.
Where is the claims department located?	Claim departments located in another state may have difficulty understanding your local reference points, resources and regulations.
What is their financial rating?	A.M. Best (www.ambest.com) assigns a rating of an insurer's financial strength. Ratings range from A++ (Superior) to S (Suspended). Use caution when an insurance company's rating drops below A-.
What is their track record for growth over the past four years?	Carriers with 20%+ growth at least 2 of the prior 3 years have a high percentage of material issues.

And always remember, one of the basic tenets of risk management is to not treat insurance as a substitute for risk control, which is the subject for the remainder of this chapter.

Risk Control

Risk control is the coordinated and economical effort to minimize the probability, frequency, severity, or unpredictability of loss. As opposed to risk financing, risk control focuses on solutions that will prevent or reduce actual harm or the cost of loss, not to provide funds to pay for losses.

We are now moving to the "Risk Management" section of our risk register, and stating our risk control solutions in the "Mitigation" column of the spreadsheet. Once risks have been identified and assessed, all techniques to manage the risk fall into one or more of these five major categories:

- Risk Avoidance (eliminates the exposure to an activity and any chance of loss)

- Loss Prevention (reduces the frequency of types of claims that cannot be eliminated)

- Loss Reduction (reduces the severity or financial impact from losses not prevented)

- Separation/Duplication (reduces overall severity)

- Risk Transfer (transfers some or all of the risk to another party)

Keep in mind that typically more than one of these strategies is appropriate, and they are quite often used in combination. For example, we may institute a training program to reduce the frequency of workplace injuries (loss prevention) and an early return-to-work program to reduce the financial impact of those injuries that do occur (loss reduction).

Following is a brief review of these strategies, along with examples of each and how they would be stated in the "Mitigation" column of your risk register. If you were clear in stating the risk in terms of its root cause, as covered in Chapter 8, then the mitigation response should be fairly straightforward. Where applicable, sources where you can obtain additional information to further develop your program are included.

Risk Avoidance

This is an informed decision to avoid activities that lead to the possibility of loss. A decision to avoid risk may mean the possibility of not earning profits as well, and it should also be noted that risk avoidance may not relieve exposure to products already in the field, or other past activities.

An example of risk avoidance would be a manufacturer who operates a fleet of trucks to deliver its products. The manufacturer may decide the control this provides in establishing its delivery schedule is not worth the liability arising out of operating heavy equipment on the highways.

To mitigate this risk, the company may state the following: "Put our product delivery business out to bid with for-hire carriers, and place all company owned equipment up for sale with a local truck dealership".

I cannot think of specific external resources on risk avoidance, as these decisions may involve conflict with the organization's other objectives, and could therefore make it difficult to gain a consensus. Consequently, these are usually debated and acted upon internally.

Loss Prevention

For those risks we cannot avoid, we institute programs designed to prevent losses. The term "prevention" implies an action taken to break the sequence of events that leads to a loss, or to make the event less likely.

An example of loss prevention is when a business implements a safety program to prevent workplace injuries. The elements can include a written safety policy, defined responsibilities and accountabilities, written programs to address hazards, and training and inspection materials.

Using one component of the above example for our risk register, where the risk was stated as, "There is a lack of clearly defined responsibilities and accountabilities for safety," the mitigation response may read, "Create safety responsibilities for all individuals including management, supervisors and line personnel."

Aside from hiring a consultant, one of the best external resources for loss prevention is insurance company safety personnel. Depending upon the types of coverages you insure, these professionals can provide expertise on a variety of loss prevention subjects, including safety and health, protection of property, fleet safety, employment practices, et cetera. In addition, more and more insurance companies have created web sites, thereby making a wealth of loss prevention information available to their insureds.

Loss Reduction

For those losses that do occur, loss reduction methods are used to reduce the severity and financial impact. These methods may involve pre-loss reduction activities or post-loss reduction activities.

Examples of pre-loss activities would be the development of a disaster recovery plan, including training and periodic testing. Post-loss reduction activities could involve claims management, including prompt claims reporting and incident investigation.

If we were going to mitigate the risk of not having a disaster recovery plan, the following statement would be appropriate in the mitigation column of our risk register: "Create a crisis management committee and develop a business continuity plan."

For additional information on business continuity planning, see the resource section at the end of this book. An early return to work program is another example of loss reduction, and these are available from your workers' compensation insurance company.

Separation/Duplication

These risk control techniques are designed to reduce high loss severity exposures, not to avoid, prevent or reduce loss to any single asset or operation.

Separation involves the isolation of an exposure from other exposures, perils, or hazards, such as when a business occupies several buildings at numerous locations rather than one large building.

Duplication entails the utilization of backups or spares, such as when a business stores its backup data at a location separate from the main place of business.

Assuming we identified the risk as, "not having spare parts on hand for our production line," we may state the mitigation as, "purchase and maintain critical spare components and store in warehouse facility separate from production building."

You may want to consider conferring with IT professionals about the most efficient way to back up your data.

Risk Transfer

This risk control technique is intended to reduce risk to the organization by transferring some or all of the risk to another party, other than an insurance company. This typically involves risk transfers by way of hold harmless, indemnity, and insurance provisions in contracts, and is also known as *contractual risk transfer*.

Examples where this technique is used include contracts with suppliers, vendors, contractors and service providers (including those servicing your premises), bailees, transportation providers, suppliers, leased employees, and lessees and renters. Of course, proof of insurance should be obtained from these other parties to assure their financial responsibility.

To mitigate the risk using this technique, we might state: "Establish a certificate of insurance program, including minimum insurance requirements, for all suppliers, contractors, etc., and maintain proof of coverage from each on an ongoing basis."

Attorney input is required as part of a contractual review process. Also, your insurance broker should be a great resource as far as reviewing the insurance requirements of a contract and providing you with input.

Here is a look at what the updated risk register would now display:

Controls	Tolerance-Decision	Mitigation
Weak: Current standard does not address consequences	Low - Treat	Create vehicle safety policy that only allows drivers with acceptable records to operate vehicles on behalf of the company
Non-existent: No procedure in place to manage certificates of insurance.	Medium - Treat	Develop certificate management procedures and assign responsibility, including training, for implementation.
Weak: No written procedure or documented tests.	Low - Treat	Write flow testing procedure and develop calendar for testing dates. Document results for all testing.
Non-existent: No plan currently in place.	Low - Treat	Create committee and develop a disaster recovery plan.
Adequate: Plan is in place but needs training	High - Monitor	Calendar for next year to review plan.

Utilizing your internal and external resources, your risk register is now almost complete. In the next chapter we will finish up with the monitoring portion of your program.

11. Monitoring Results

"An organization's ability to learn, and translate that learning into action rapidly, is the ultimate competitive advantage"

Jack Welch

A good management system includes the ability to continuously track and evaluate progress in order to make any necessary adjustments in plans that were made. That is the purpose of this stage of the risk management process, and can be accomplished by measuring results, activities completed, or both.

Measuring results would include tracking incidents that occurred or losses that were incurred. This could be done using a risk management information system, or by periodically requesting claims history updates from the insurance company. The disadvantage of relying on results measurements is that they occur after the fact, and don't take the element of luck into consideration. In other words, just because something did not go wrong does not mean anything was done to mitigate the risk from occurring – perhaps we were just lucky.

Activities, on the other hand, are easily measured and provide accountability for completing the agreed upon risk mitigation strategies. The risk register serves as an excellent tool for monitoring the activity aspect of our program by documenting the name(s) of those who take ownership for each risk, the status of their progress in mitigating the risk, and a projected date for completion.

Ownership

This is one of the more powerful sections, as it puts accountability into the process. Ownership can be assigned to an individual, a responsible team, or a combination of internal personnel and external resources, like a subject matter expert, when necessary.

Status/Remarks

The status column allows you to make periodic comments on the progress of each risk mitigation project.

Date

Date, like ownership, places accountability by displaying the deadline established for the completion of the risk mitigation project.

As mentioned earlier, you may define other columns in the risk register to suit your business needs. For example, you may want to insert a column for departments or divisions, or you can dedicate a column for articulating your risk financing solutions. Any additional information that allows you to sort and analyze your data, or provides clarification on the risk, should be taken into consideration.

The balance of our example risk register with these areas filled in is displayed:

Mitigation	Owner	Status /Remarks	Date
Create vehicle safety policy that only allows drivers with acceptable records to operate vehicles on behalf of the company	G. Clooney	In progress	10-Dec
Develop certificate management procedures and assign responsibility, including training, for implementation.	T. Hanks	In progress	7-Dec
Write flow testing procedure and develop calendar for testing dates. Document results for all testing.	J. Wayne	Completed	23-Mar
Create committee and develop a disaster recovery plan.	J. Wayne	In progress	25-May
Calendar for next year to review plan.	S. Bullock	Suspended	10-Oct

Congratulations! You have now been through all four steps in the risk management process, documented your progress, and completed the plan. However, you are not finished. Recall from Chapter 6 that risk management is a continuous process, so what has really been accomplished on this first pass is establishing a foundation to build upon. In order to keep the risk management program alive and well, here are some tips for going forward:

1. Meet on a regular basis to review progress on the mitigation of risks.

2. Update rankings to existing risks as conditions change.

3. Encourage team members to identify new risks to be added to the risk register, and always assume the list of considered risks, no matter how extensive, is incomplete.

4. Strike through (do not delete) risks for which mitigation is complete.

When change that requires a revision to the risk register takes place be sure to create an updated version, and archive the previous ones for future reference. This not only documents your efforts, it provides a valuable reference when looking back and gauging the effectiveness of your program as well.

You can also copy and paste your top ten or twenty risks into a PowerPoint™ presentation that can be used for succinctly reporting to your board of directors in support of their governance and oversight responsibilities.

Risk management is a *people process*, in that people must be involved in all aspects of an effective risk management program. I have learned from experience in consulting on these types of projects that a number of elements must be in place to assure the team advances in the desired direction. In the next, and final, chapter we will discuss how to administer your program in order to make it a success.

Simpler is Better

I attended the annual conference of the Risk and Insurance Management Society in Boston, MA one year. Over the course of four days, between seminar sessions, I trekked through the massive exhibit hall where vendors were displaying everything related to risk, including some cool risk management software.

Now I am not good at technology, but I found it fascinating to see the problems it can solve and the time it can save. The various demonstrations I attended displayed neat looking dashboards, graphs, charts and reports that can assist an organization in its risk management efforts. My tote bag was getting full of brochures from numerous software providers, and the more questions I asked the more complex these systems seemed to be. On the third day, I became convinced that these risk management software programs were really only for big companies.

On the fourth day, I attended a two hour session put on by the risk manager of the largest technology company in the world. They do business in170 countries, employ 304,000 people, and have 88,000 retail locations. After explaining their risk management program, it was time for Q & A. One of the questions was about the software they used to run their risk management program. I was amazed at the answer, Microsoft Excel™ and PowerPoint™, with no plans to make any changes. Perhaps simpler is better.

12. Administering Your Program

"Management is nothing more than motivating other people"

Lee Iacocca

Recall Chapter 8, in which we discussed the failure of management systems due to company standards, policies and administrative control issues, or the lack of use thereof. This holds true for risk management systems as well, so this chapter will discuss some of the components you will want to consider as part of administering your program to assure success. These include a mission statement, a policy statement and a procedure manual, all with support from demonstrated management leadership.

Risk Management Mission Statement

A risk management mission statement provides the framework or context within which the company's risk management strategies are formulated. It should accurately explain why your program exists and what it hopes to achieve in the future. By relating your risk management mission statement to the corporate mission, it also demonstrates support for achieving the organization's objectives.

The preparation of a risk management mission statement should be a group project. Hopefully this undertaking will involve individuals at various levels of the organization, including those involved in risk management. The following are a couple of examples of risk management mission statements.

Example 1

The Mission of our company's risk management program is to consistently inform management of risk issues facing the Company, its assets, and its employees.

To treat risks with the methods most beneficial, economical, feasible and sensible for the safety, security and integrity of the Company and its partners – our employees, directors, shareholders, customers, vendors, and the communities we serve.

The benchmark for measuring the success of the Company's risk management program will be the analysis of the "total cost of risk".

Example 2

The Mission of the risk management function and program is to plan, organize, and direct the activities of the Company in order to minimize the adverse effects of accidental losses, at a reasonable cost.

Risk management applies to all aspects of our operations that can potentially cause loss to our customers, employees and property, wherever located. This includes our liability arising from contracts, products and services we sell, and the property we own. Also included are losses to our plant, equipment, products before sale, monies and other valuables of the Company.

The benchmark for measuring the success of the Company's risk management program will be a combination of risk mitigation activities and our total cost of risk.

Finally, it is a good practice to make sure that people within the organization, as well as the different constituencies that the organization hopes to affect, are all aware of the risk management mission statement.

Risk Management Policy Statement

Policies are statements about how different types of activities will be performed, and serve to protect an organization from misunderstandings that might lead to unauthorized behavior or lawsuits.

The risk management policy statement should give an overview of the policy and why it was created. The main purpose of a policy statement is to avoid confusion by clearly specifying responsibilities and authority, to open up lines of communication, and to minimize duplication of effort. Following is an example of a risk management policy statement:

Example

ABC Company recognizes its responsibility to the public, its employees and its stockholders to safeguard persons, products, and property by every reasonable means.

Therefore, it is our policy to fix staff responsibility for the administration of our risk management program with the Finance Department. Line management is still accountable for implementing procedures and policies. Line managers are expected to recommend changes, and make comments about the effectiveness of these policies and procedures, to the Finance Department.

The Finance Department shall have responsibility for:

   a.   Allocating insurance premiums and other risk costs to Subsidiaries, Departments and other cost centers;

   b.   Selecting all risk management services, including brokers, claims adjusters, loss prevention services, and consultants;

c.   Adjusting all major losses and claims;

d.   Maintaining accurate records of all losses, claims, insurance premiums and other risk-related expenses; and

e.   Coordinating and accounting for all of the Company's risk-related expenses.

The CFO will evaluate the Company's risks and determine whether to assume or insure these risks. In the performance of this task, the CFO shall select appropriate deductibles and limits of insurance. The CFO will use self-insurance programs where beneficial to the Company.

The CFO will be a member of the Risk Management Committee, stay fully informed on the Company's exposures, and maintain adequate data to assess the program's performance.

The Risk Management Committee shall provide assistance to the Board of Directors in fulfilling its responsibilities for risk oversight, and is constituted to assist the Board in the discharge of its duties and responsibilities in this regard.

(*see sample risk management committee charter in Appendix C*).

Risk Management Procedures Manual

The risk management procedures manual should provide a basic outline of the insurance and self-insurance programs put in place by the Finance Department. It should also include procedures that relate to the management of risk.

As a guide, the manual should help line management and operating personnel address issues related to the business's risks and the program to protect against them. Through better knowledge of insurance coverage, claims procedures, risk information, and safe practices, the organization will realize a reduction in the number and amount of losses. This knowledge will help safeguard customers, employees, and the communities in which the organization operates, while adding to company earnings.

The purposes of this manual are to:

1. Establish company's position on the management of the risks of accidental loss (fire, liability, etc.);

2. Provide information for the reporting of claims arising from the company's operations;

3. Set forth procedures for regular reporting on operations and exposures to accidental loss; and

4. Define procedures for activities that present risks of loss to the company and its insurance program.

An example of the table of contents from a risk management procedure manual I have successfully used with clients for many years is included in Appendix F.

Leadership

The most important element in any business undertaking is management support. Management must exhibit leadership when it comes to risk management by integrating risk management into the business practice. In other words, risk management should be part of the business, not in addition to the business.

Researchers have observed five broad functions a leader performs when promoting the organization's effectiveness. These functions include: (1) environmental monitoring, (2) organizing subordinate activities, (3) teaching and coaching subordinates, (4) motivating others, and (5) intervening actively in the group's work. Leadership is ultimately about creating a way for people to contribute to making something extraordinary happen.

I have shared some stories in this book about my experience of successes and failures in working with organizations to implement risk management programs. In every case, leadership, or lack thereof, made the difference in the outcome of these projects.

Putting it All Together

I hope the examples and stories shared throughout this book help paint a clear picture of how to implement your risk management strategy. Start out easy, perhaps focusing on one category or even a specific area of risk. You will soon learn how well this augments your business planning and enhances internal communication.

You may also want to periodically visit our web site at www.RiskSkillsCenter.com, where new training videos, documents, and other useful information will be continually updated.

Throughout this book I have emphasized risk control measures as they relate to a balanced risk management program. However, my intention has not been to undermine the importance of insurance as the other measure of balance. Therefore, I am going to end with one more story that goes back to the beginning of my career, and serves as one of my earliest lessons in insurance.

The Cute Sisters

It was November of 1971 and I working for an insurance agency, selling automobile and homeowners insurance policies. Fresh out of college, my insurance training consisted of completing a licensing course and attending a couple of insurance company sponsored product seminars. I had three months' experience under my belt and I was ready to go.

I contacted a client of the agency for whom we handled automobile insurance, and asked if we could meet to discuss the possibility of also handling his homeowners insurance. We set the appointment for one evening the following week as the current homeowners policy was coming due for renewal soon.

When I arrived for our appointment I was met by a very nice young couple who were clearly proud of their home. The house was one year old and I was impressed by how nicely they had landscaped the yard and furnished the interior. My guided tour included a peek in the garage to see their new Buick Riviera, with light metallic green paint and a dark green vinyl top. I also got to meet their two cute young daughters, of whom they were equally proud.

As we sat around the oak dining room table, I evaluated their current policy and calculated the appropriate amount of coverage it would take to rebuild the house if it were destroyed. Referencing what I had learned during my limited training, I pointed out that their current amount of coverage was inadequate to rebuild the home. I then calculated the premium we would charge for providing a policy with the appropriate amount of coverage, and they were clearly disappointed at the additional cost over what they were currently paying.

It took a fair amount of conversation to convince them to buy the more expensive policy, and I was excited when they decided to place the coverage with our agency. I had made one of my first sales.

Eleven days later the call came into our insurance agency. There was a fire at the home and the wife was reporting a claim. I was told by the agency owner to drive out to the house and meet with our customer and the insurance company adjuster as a sign of support. I was shocked when I saw what was left of the structure; the fireplace at one end and one half of the garage at the other end, with the charred remains of the Riviera inside. What I will never forget was seeing the husband mowing the lawn in front of this pile of rubble – he was clearly in shock.

It turned out my calculations were correct, and there was just enough insurance to rebuild the house, replace the furnishings, and even pay for the damaged landscape. This early lesson taught me about the importance of insurance, as well as taking the time to plan for the right amount of coverage. Oh, by the way, the cause of the fire was due to the two sisters. They had been told not to play with daddy's lighter, so they went into their bedroom closet to light it, catching the hanging clothes on fire. The conflagration quickly spread to the attic and then throughout the house. I am pretty certain they learned a lesson as well.

Conclusion

I hope this book helps you establish a risk management program for your organization. While there are many benefits to be derived from doing so, you must allow some time for the process to mature. By adopting the concepts presented in this book, and following the steps outlined herein, you will soon be able to:

1. Define your board and executives' risk-related responsibilities in conjunction with a risk management committee;

2. Formalize your organization's management of risk by adopting a process upon which you can base your related activities;

3. Customize your activity to correspond with your particular risk imperatives, your industry and your key strategies;

4. Utilize in-house or outsourced expertise to assist in implementation;

5. Document your plan to improve reporting and governance.

Start by taking one step at a time and focusing on a narrow range of risks. As you gain familiarity, and confidence, you will find that the process moves more quickly and efficiently.

Be sure to check back at our web site, www.RiskSkillsCenter.com, from time to time for new programs and additional resources to help your organization reduce uncertainty in achieving its objectives. You can also contact me directly at ed@kempkey.com. I hope to hear from you.

About the Author

Ed Kempkey is the founder of Risk Skills Center and CEO of Kempkey Insurance Services, Inc., a commercial insurance brokerage firm that he founded in 1980. Prior to starting his own company, Ed was vice-president of underwriting for an insurance company, after which he moved on to become president of a large multi-location insurance agency.

While insurance is an important element in protecting the assets of an organization, Ed also recognizes that it does not cover all costs of accidental losses, nor is it a substitute for good risk management practices. He believes that in the long run, the only answer to reducing the total cost of risk, whether insured or otherwise handled, is to reduce or control losses.

By going beyond insurance, Ed utilizes a flexible, yet comprehensive, approach in developing an effective risk management program that provides long term, sustainable cost containment strategies. He has adopted an international standard as the basis for a process that identifies and assesses organizations risks, then creates a plan for treating the most critical risks in a cost effective manner.

Ed has presented numerous seminars on a variety of risk management topics including safety and health, enterprise risk management, accident investigation, business continuity planning, and human resource related subjects. Many of his seminars have been approved for continuing education credits by the Society for Human Resource Management.

In addition to public seminars, Ed also conducts on-site training for managers and supervisors to support their role in protecting the organization. Each training module covers a different law that imposes personal liability for their responsibility in supervising others, and educates them to recognize it when a situation arises and how to properly respond.

Ed's picture has appeared on the front cover of a national risk management magazine in connection with a story on his work with the wine industry. He also writes a weekly newsletter titled "risKey" on a variety of insurance and risk management topics, and is the author of the Risk Management Procedures Guide, a complete manual covering all aspects of administering a risk management program. Professional affiliations include the Risk and Insurance Management Society, and the Professional Risk Managers International Association.

Ed is an experienced pilot and enjoys flying for pleasure and business. He holds a commercial pilot's license with multi-engine and instrument ratings. In addition to flying, he enjoys riding his motorcycle on the back roads of the California North Coast.

Appendix A: Glossary

Exposure – the state of being subject to loss because of some hazard or contingency. Also used as a measure of the rating units or the premium base of a risk.

Hazard – a condition within an exposure that may give rise to an incident or increase the likelihood of a loss from a given peril (physical, moral, or morale). **Peril** – the cause of a loss, e.g., fire, windstorm, collision.

Incident – an event that disrupts normal activities and may become a loss.

Accident – an unplanned event, definite as to time and place, that results in injury or damage to a person or property.

Occurrence – an accident with the limitation of time removed (an "accident" that is extended over a period of time, rather than a single observable happening).

Loss – a reduction in the value of assets.

Claim – a demand for payment of an obligation resulting from a loss.

Frequency – the number of losses occurring in a given time period.

Severity – the dollar amount of a given loss, or the aggregate dollar amount of all losses for a given period.

Expected losses – projection of the frequency or severity of losses based on loss history, probability distributions, and statistics.

Appendix B: Cost of Risk Worksheet

	General Liability	Commercial Auto	Property	Workers Comp
Cost of your premiums:				
Cost of your deductibles:	+	+	+	+
Direct, but uncovered, cost of your claims:	+	+	+	+
Indirect, but uncovered, cost of your claims:	+	+	+	+
Your estimated total cost of risk:	$	$	$	$

Appendix C: Risk Management Committee Charter

Purpose

The Risk Management Committee (the "Committee") shall provide assistance to the Board of Directors in fulfilling its responsibility for risk oversight, and is constituted to assist the Board in the discharge of its duties and responsibilities in this regard.

Membership

The Committee shall be composed of at least two Directors. The members of the Committee shall be appointed by the Board and shall serve until such member's successor is duly elected and qualified, or until such member's earlier resignation or removal. The members of the Committee may be removed, with or without cause, by a majority vote of the Board.

Chairman

Unless a Chairman is elected by the Board, the members of the Committee shall designate a Chairman by majority vote of the full Committee membership. The Chairman will chair all regular sessions of the Committee and set the agenda for Committee meetings.

Meetings

The Committee shall meet at least four times per annum. The Chairman of the Committee, or a majority of the permanent members of the Committee, may convene additional meetings as circumstances may dictate.

Responsibility

The Committee is responsible for:

1. Identifying and measuring all business risks affecting the conduct of the Company;

2. Assessing risks in order to make informed decisions on how to respond;

3. Implementing the best solutions for controlling risks; and

4. Monitoring the results of the risk management program.

Authority

The Committee shall have the authority to obtain inside or outside professional advice, and to secure the attendance of insiders or outsiders with relevant experience and expertise, as it deems necessary.

Reporting

The Committee reports directly to the Board.

Appendix D: Risk Register

Risk Identification		Risk Assessment						Risk Management			
Risk Category	Risk Statement	L	C	Score	Rank	Existing Controls	Tolerance-Decision	Mitigation	Owner	Status/Remarks	Date

Appendix E: Risk Categories

Financial Risks

Interest rate
Foreign exchange
Commodity
Equity
Weather
Business cycles
Seasonal risks
Price, margin management
Competition, market characteristics
Consumer change
Depression
Inflation
Political unrest
Stock market swings
Technology advances
War
Terrorism

Strategic Risks

Customers
Products
Channels
Competitors
Regulatory
Geopolitical

Operational Risks

Supply chain
Business interruption

Operational Risks continued

Brand
Reputation
Corporate image
Human resources
Disease
    Drug addition
    Smoking
    Alcoholism
    Obesity
Epidemic
    Influenza
Death
Obsolescence
Civil rights
Independent contractors
Family members
Resignation
Termination
Retirement
Business continuation agreements
Overseas
Kidnap

Hazard Risks

Industrial injuries
Safety
Legal/environmental
Property
Owned property
Leased & hired property

Dependencies – major customers
Dependencies – key suppliers
Business stoppage – delay
Critical equipment or site
Other interruption – injunction, curfew, etc.
Network failure

Records, files, archives
Vehicles
Property under construction
Vacant or closed property
Intellectual property, trade secrets
Goods in transit
Others goods in our care custody
Shared assets, joint venture
Cash
Valuables – fine arts, etc.

Liability Risks

Third party liabilities
    Advertisers
    Athletic sponsorship
    Automobile liability (owned, non-owned, repossessed, trust)
    Aircraft liability (owned, non-owned, repossessed, trust)
Bailee liability
    Goods of others
    Manuscripts
    Parking areas
    Specifications
    Exhibitions
Broadcasters
Publishers
Conflict of interest
Contractual liability
    Lease agreements
    Sales or purchase orders
    Notes, mortgages, loans
    Construction contracts
    Property of others in care or custody

Natural Risks

Collapse
Corrosion
Drought
Earthquake
Erosion
Fire
Flood
Hail
Ice
Landslides
Lightning
Subsidence
Temperature changes
Tides
Vegetation
Volcanoes
Water
Wind

Liability Risks (cont'd)
Insurance contracts (warranties or conditions)
Directors & Officers liability (wrongful acts)
Employers' liability
Workers' compensation laws (all states)
U.S. Longshoreman's & Harborworker's Act
Jones Act (seaman)
Foreign (repatriation, etc.)
Occupational Safety & Health Act (OSHA)
Employee benefit plan liability
Environmental pollution liability
Equal employment Opportunity liability
Liquor law liability (Dram Shop Act)

Safety and Health Risks

Management leadership
Accountability, responsibility, & authority
Employee participation
Hazard assessment & control
Employee information & training
Incident investigation

Workers' Compensation Risks

Claims reporting
Claims management
Medical provider
Early return to work

Employment Issues List

Hiring
Screening
Orientation
Job descriptions
Performance evaluation
Discipline
Recordkeeping
Termination
COBRA
Grievances
Leave of absences
Management rights
Medical records
Open door
Personnel records (access to)
Sexual harassment
Discrimination

OSHA Compliance Risks

IIPP program
Hazard identification
Accident investigation
Training
Recordkeeping
Safety committee

Appendix F: Risk Management Procedures Manual

Here is a sample table of contents for a risk management procedures manual. Note that each of the coverages in the insurance coverage section also include a brief description, policy information, and claims procedure.

Table of Contents

Section 1 – Introduction

Section 2 – Insurance Coverage

General Liability
Automobile Liability
Automobile Physical Damage
Workers' Compensation & Employers Liability
Excess Coverage
Liquor Liability
International
Employment Practices Liability
Fiduciary
Employee Benefits Liability
Directors and Officers Liability
Environmental/Pollution Liability
Property
Electronic Data Processing Equipment (EDP)
Fine Arts
Earthquake
Property in Transit – Land
Property in Transit – Ocean
Employee Dishonesty
Surety Bonds

Section 3 – Contracts and Certificates

Procedures for Contracts
Contracts: Hold Harmless Clauses
Contracts: Insurance Clauses
Certificates of Insurance
Internal Certificate Management Procedure

Section 4 – Loss Control

Safety
Responsibilities for Supporting Safety
Safety and Fire Protection
How to Get Ready to Instruct
Job Instruction Training
Safety Committee and Safety Meetings
Inspections

Accident Investigation and Reports

Section 5 – Government Regulations

OSHA – Injury Prevention Program
References
Workplace Violence
Responsibilities for Prevention Program
Americans with Disabilities Act (FMLA)
Family and Medical Leave Act (ADA)
Equal Employment Opportunity
Sexual Harassment
      References

Section 6 – General Procedures

Workers' Comp Early Return to Work Program
Use of Company Vehicles
Personal Automobile Use
Employee Use of the Internet
Travel
Air Travel
Car Rentals
Rental or Leasing of Aircraft/Watercraft
Sponsored & Special Events
Handling of Funds
Security Procedures

Section 7 – Exposure & Activity Reporting

Operations Informational Reporting
Safety Activity Reporting
Section 8 – Exhibits

Risk Management Committee Agenda
Approved List of Contractors
Approved List of Drivers
Insurance Requirements from Suppliers, Vendors, etc.

Appendix G: Resources

There are many excellent sources of information scattered throughout the web that will provide you with more information about managing risk. This is a short list of web sites you might find especially interesting:

Agility Recovery http://www2.agilityrecovery.com/

Agility Recovery Solutions is a former division of GE with 21 years' disaster recovery and business continuity experience. They are dedicated to creating and delivering innovative business continuity solutions that challenge traditional industry barriers of scale, cost and complexity. As such, they provide comprehensive, packaged recovery solutions, consulting services and testing options to businesses across the United States and Canada.

BISIMPLIFIED http://www.bisimplifed.com

This completely interactive Business Interruption web site provides all essential business interruption information in a user friendly, simplified format. Business professionals who subscribe find it combines the latest technology with straightforward examples and explanations that inform, instruct, and END THE CONFUSION.

Bureau of Labor Statistics http://www.bls.gov/

The Bureau of Labor Statistics of the U.S. Department of Labor is the principal Federal agency responsible for measuring labor market activity, working conditions, and price changes in the economy. Its mission is to collect, analyze, and disseminate essential economic information to support public and private decision making. As an independent statistical agency, BLS serves its diverse user communities by providing products and services that are objective, timely, accurate, and relevant.

Disaster Assistance

http://www.disasterassistance.gov/disasterinformation/index.shtm

DisasterAssistance.gov provides information on how you might be able to get help from the U.S. government before, during and after a disaster. DisasterAssistance.gov also provides news, information and resources to prepare for disasters, help keep your family safe during an emergency, and recover afterwards.

Emergency Management Guide for Business and Industry

http://www.fema.gov/pdf/business/guide/bizindst.pdf

This guide provides a step by step approach to emergency planning, response and recovery for companies of all sizes. I have used it many times to facilitate the development of business contingency plans for my clients.

Insurance Information Institute http://www.iii.org/

The mission of the Insurance Information Institute (I.I.I.) is to improve public understanding of insurance — what it does and how it works. For more than 40 years, the I.I.I. has provided definitive insurance information. Today, the I.I.I. is recognized by the media, governments, regulatory organizations, universities and the public as a primary source of information, analysis and referral concerning insurance. Each year, the I.I.I. works on more than 3,700 news stories, handles more than 6,000 requests for information and answers nearly 50,000 questions from consumers. They also publish a host of helpful pamphlets and books on insurance subjects.

ISO 31000 Principles and Guidelines

http://www.iso.org/iso/catalogue_detail.htm?csnumber=43170

ISO (International Organization for Standardization) is the world's largest developer and publisher of International Standards. They are a network of the national standards institutes of 163 countries, one member per country, with a Central Secretariat in Geneva, Switzerland that coordinates the system.

ISO is a non-governmental organization that forms a bridge between the public and private sectors. On the one hand, many of its member institutes are part of the governmental structure of their countries, or are mandated by their governments. On the other hand, other members have their roots uniquely in the private sector, having been set up by national partnerships of industry associations.

Therefore, ISO enables a consensus to be reached on solutions that meet both the requirements of business and the broader needs of society.

National Highway Traffic Safety Administration

http://www.nhtsa.gov/

NHTSA was established by the Highway Safety Act of 1970 to carry out safety programs previously administered by the National Highway Safety Bureau. Specifically, the agency directs the highway safety and consumer programs established by the National Traffic and Motor Vehicle Safety Act of 1966, the Highway Safety Act of 1966, the 1972 Motor Vehicle Information and Cost Savings Act, and succeeding amendments to these laws. Dedicated to achieving the highest standards of excellence in motor vehicle and highway safety, NHTSA works daily to help prevent crashes and their attendant costs, both human and financial. The agency strives to exceed the expectations of its customers through its core values of integrity, service, and leadership

National Safety Council http://www.nsc.org/Pages/Home.aspx

The National Safety Council saves lives by preventing injuries and deaths at work, in homes and communities, and on the roads through leadership, research, education and advocacy.

By 2014, the council will save an additional 10,000 lives and prevent 1 million injuries. To achieve this goal, it will continue to partner with businesses, elected officials and the public to make an impact in areas such as distracted driving, teen driving, workplace safety, and safety in the home and community.

The Council encourages businesses and individuals to get involved, and provides a variety of ways to do so. Check out the Get Involved (http://www.nsc.org/get_involved/Pages/Home.aspx) section of the web site.

Workplace safety and transportation have been critical areas of focus to the Council since its inception in 1913. Over the years, increases in unintentional injury and death rates in homes and communities have resulted in the Council expanding its focus to include safety in homes and communities.

Network of Employers for Traffic Safety http://trafficsafety.org/

The Network of Employers for Traffic Safety is an employer-led, public/private partnership dedicated to improving the safety and health of employees, their families, and members of the communities in which they live and work by preventing traffic crashes that occur both on and off the job.

OSHA Ratio of Indirect to Direct Costs
http://www.osha.gov/dcsp/smallbusiness/safetypays/background.html

This is part of the Federal OSHA's Safety Pays Program.

Public Risk Management Association
http://www.primacentral.org/index.cfm

Provides programs, education, and services to support the public risk management profession.

Ready Business http://www.ready.gov/business/

The U.S. Department of Homeland Security and the Advertising Council launched the *Ready Business* Campaign in September 2004. This extension of the successful *Ready* Campaign, designed to educate and empower Americans to prepare for and respond to emergencies, focuses specifically on business preparedness. *Ready Business* helps owners and managers of small- and medium-sized businesses prepare their employees, operations and assets for the possibility of an emergency.

Risk and Insurance Management Society www.rims.org

The Risk and Insurance Management Society, Inc. (RIMS) is a not-for-profit organization dedicated to advancing the practice of risk management. Founded in 1950, RIMS represents more than 3,500 industrial, service, nonprofit, charitable and governmental entities. The Society serves more than 10,000 risk management professionals around the world.

Risk Management Guide for Information Technology Systems
http://csrc.nist.gov/publications/nistpubs/800-30/sp800-30.pdf

This Guide includes recommendations of the National Institute of Standards and Technology for computer security.

The Federal Motor Carrier Safety Administration's Safety Analysis Program for Commercial Drivers
http://csa2010.fmcsa.dot.gov/

Compliance, Safety, Accountability (CSA) is a Federal Motor Carrier Safety Administration (FMCSA) initiative to improve large truck and bus safety, and ultimately reduce crashes, injuries, and fatalities related to commercial motor vehicles. It introduces a new enforcement and compliance model that allows FMCSA and its state partners to contact a larger number of carriers earlier, in order to address safety problems before crashes occur. Rolled out in December 2010, the program establishes a new nationwide system for making the roads safer for motor carriers and the public alike.

The Institute for Business & Home Safety
http://www.disastersafety.org/

The Institute for Business & Home Safety's mission is to reduce the social and economic effects of natural disasters and other property losses by conducting research and advocating improved construction, maintenance and preparation practices.

The Institute of Risk Management   http://www.theirm.org/

The Institute of Risk Management (IRM) is the world's leading enterprise-wide risk education Institute. It is an independent, well-respected advocate of the risk profession, owned by practicing risk professionals. IRM passionately believes in the importance of risk management and that investment in education and continual professional development leads to more effective risk management. It provides qualifications, short courses and events at a range of levels from introductory to expert. IRM supports risk professionals by providing the skills and tools needed to put theory into practice in order to deal with the demands of a constantly changing, sophisticated and challenging business environment. It operates internationally, with members and students in over 50 countries, drawn from a variety of risk-related disciplines and a wide range of industries.

The Wausau Multiline Productivity Poll

http://www.riskandinsurance.com/userpdfs//2007WausauMultilinePro
dPoll.pdf

The Wausau Multiline Productivity Poll is a survey report about efficiency trends across major lines of commercial insurance, including identification of the real cost of risk.

U.S. Computer Emergency Readiness Team, part of the U.S. Department of Homeland Security http://www.us-cert.gov/

US-CERT is charged with providing response support and defense against cyber attacks for the Federal Civil Executive Branch (.gov), and information sharing and collaboration with state and local government, industry and international partners.

US-CERT interacts with federal agencies, industry, the research community, state and local governments, and others to disseminate reasoned and actionable cyber security information to the public.

U.S. Small Business Administration http://www.sba.gov/

The U.S. Small Business Administration (SBA) dedicates its energy and resources to providing support to small businesses and small business owners across the nation. SBA helps businesses across the country through the "3 C's" of its service:

- **Capital:** The SBA works with about 5,000 banks to provide SBA loans to deserving small businesses.

- **Contracts:** The SBA works to ensure that 23% of federal contract dollars go to small businesses.

- **Counseling:** 14,000 SBA-affiliated counselors are ready when you need small business guidance.

The web site also contains a lot of information about starting and managing a business.